Kathak Yog

Poetry of Dance and Immersion

Dr. Patrali Chakrabarty

BookLeaf Publishing

India | USA | UK

Made with ❤ on the BookLeaf Publishing Platform
www.bookleafpub.in
www.bookleafpub.com

Dedication

This book is dedicated to the Chakrabartys -

Parents, who sowed the seed of discovering bliss everywhere.

Tapan Kumar Chakrabarty (Baba): You have my head and heart. I love you every day.

Dipa Chakrabarty (Ma): You instilled in me the seed of unwavered faith.

Brother - Dr. Saurish Chakrabarty - Thank you for loving with all your heart.

Daughter - Shriya Chakraborty, my constant source of bliss and motivation. Thank you for the constant and much needed constructive criticism, during the developmental phase of this book.

My Teachers -

Guruji - Pt. Rajendra Gangani. You are my ephemeral Guru. Blessed to have found you in this life.

Yogacharya Simon Gill - I know you are in eternal peace Sir. Thank you for the healing. Pranam.

My God. Me. Kathak. Bharatvarsh. Everything that has touched my life in various ways, to make me who I am today.

Thank you.

.

Acknowledgement

With deep gratitude, I acknowledge my fellow dancers, musicians, and yogis, who have enriched this journey. Your passion ignites inspiration through every verse.

A special thanks to my mentors, who constantly help me steer through the depths of Kathak, Music, Yog, and Bhakti.

I extend my heartfelt thanks to the timeless wisdom of the Bhagavad Gita, Natya Shastra by Bharat Muni, works of Kabiguru Rabindranath Tagore, whose teachings have profoundly influenced my journey.

To the dancers, yogis, and seekers of truth – may this book guide you through spiritual immersions during Riyaaz, connecting the heart of movement, sound, and devotion, to add bliss to your journey.

Anandohum!

Preface

This book is an account of my journey into the arduous but ultimately blissful realms of Kathak Yog. This is the book of "Pranamaya KathakYog" - The book of Prana - effervescent energy, and divine spirit. With every poem the Yogi delves into different facets of Kathak, while discovering exciting dimensions of spirituality. This book will be an exploration for all readers, whether initiated or uninitiated to Kathak.

The poetry unfolds in two sections:
1) A set of Kavitt and Kavitangi Paran – poetry as used in rhythmic Kathak words and syllables. These poems are written essentially in Hindi using sounds of the Tabla and Pakhawaj. Every such poem is then followed by a poetic translation (in English) of the same. The translated poem, eventhough a standalone piece, narrates the thoughts behind the rhythmic syllables that the Kavitt originally portrays in its Hindi form.

2) The second section is poems written in English, but often interspersed with words or phrases that are originally from the fields of Kathak and Yoga. I have used this space to provide an introduction to the seminal thoughts that have driven the beautiful idea of Kathak Yog as a concept.

Finally, I have reserved the last bit of this book to provide brief definitions of terminologies that will appear throughout the poetry in here, but are specific to Kathak and Yog, for readers who are new to either concept of Kathak or Yog. Visit the last Chapter "A Glimpse into the KathakYog Glossary", whenever you come across something unfamiliar while travelling through this piece.

"Katha kahe so Kathak kahave" – The one who narrates tales (katha) is a Kathak. The term Kathak therefore is used to depict both the art and the artist. Various theories exist about where this divine artform was originally conceived in. In its present form, most of the elements of Kathak have come from India, especially the Northern and Western parts of its ancient undivided (akhand) state. However, some prominent elements of the dance form, like continuous spins ("*chakkar*"), entry pieces ("*Amad*"), reflect Persian practices and dance/prayer rituals.

Kathak has been hailed from ancient times as an artform of travelling storytellers, who narrated beautiful tales of the Gods as well as religious lores as skits and dance drama. This beautiful artform abides by most principles of Bharat Muni's Natya Shastra, while also allowing immense creative freedom to the practitioner, thus making the Kathak more and more versatile with each passing day.

Yog / Yoga, on the other hand, simply translated means "Union". It can imply the union between the Yogi's mind and body. It can be the union between the Yogi's mind and their inner spirit. It can be the union between the Yogi's inner spirit and their divine creator

/ the Supreme Lord / the Supreme Spirit. If you blend this with the beautiful concept of non-duality (Advaitah), captured in Poem #6 (Section 2), Yog is the union between a Yogi and every other entity - themselves, their fellow beings, nature, the universe, and the Divine Lord. Everything blends into one. The microcosm, the macrocosm, everything known and unknown – become one, thus attaining divine bliss at the lotus feet of the beautiful, divine creator.

The term "Kathak Yog" was coined to capture the essence of a Kathak's attainment of perfect bliss. The mini *samadhi* that a Kathak can feel every time during rigorous and disciplined practice (*riyaaz*), creates a replica of Yog – between the Kathak and the divine presence. Throughout this book, the poet has shared this experience of bliss and realization. Thank you for connecting with me through this piece and I hope you feel the bliss of rendezvous with the divine through every poem. Aum! Peace!

Table of Contents

Section 3: Glossary

Section 1: Kavitt

This section presents nine *Kavitt* and *Kavitangi Paran.*

A *Kavitt* is a stylized Kathak poem that uses words and additional rhythmic syllables depicting the sounds of the Tabla.

A *Kavitangi Paran,* on the other hand is a stylized Kathak poem as well, but mostly engaging heavier and sometimes more baritone-heavy rhythmic syllables that originate from the Pakhawaj.

The Taal (cyclical rhythmic template) that the Kavitt reads best in is also mentioned at the start of each one. A glossary of the Taal's used has been included in Chapter 2 of Section 3, for easier understanding.

The generic language although in Hindi, the Kavitt are written using the English script to accommodate all lovers of Kathak. Each poem is also followed with a poetic translation of the same in the English language. Therefore, you will find 18 poems in this section including both the Kavitt/Kavitangi Paran and their individual translated poems.

Here's to great beginnings!

1. Nataraj Paran

[Taal: Dhamar, 14 matra, Madhya Laya, see
Glossary: Taal]

Nataraj Natadev Nateshwar
Shambho Swayambho ||

Drig drig drig drig Dug dug dug dug
Nirat karat Tandav Tridev Mahadev ||

Chandra lalaat karpoor chhata sohe
Tat dhilam Tat dhilam Dha Mahadev ||

Drimi drimi madh madh Taranga uth
Ardh anga sadhe Laasya Nirali ||
Ta thei ta thei ta thei
Dhinaka takita Dhrum Chhanda sawari ||

Dhet tari kit taka thei Dhe tari kit taka thei
Tarikit thei Tarikit thei Tarikit Tarikit Tarikit
Thei - 1 2
Dhet tari kit taka thei Dhe tari kit taka thei
Tarikit thei Tarikit thei Tarikit Tarikit Tarikit
Thei - 1 2
Dhet tari kit taka thei Dhe tari kit taka thei
Tarikit thei Tarikit thei Tarikit Tarikit Tarikit ||
Thei X

2. Nataraj: The Lord of Dance {Translated}

In a place that is nowhere, stands
magnanimity himself.
Nataraj: His dance – incessant,
His rhythm – the pulse of creation.

From him emerge divine melodies and
movements.
The sounds of his Damaru enchant.
They sync to his motion,
They sync to his stillness.

Their Eyes open and then shut tight as they
swing
To his ceaseless cosmic dance.
We bow to the alluring symphony of the end
and rebirth.

A flash, a tap, a sizzle –
Flames enrapture the silence of creation.
The silver sliver moon sits humble on his
striking brow.

The shimmer of infinite grace and beauty!

Gently and sweetly the rhythms send ripples
and waves
Revealing the other side of his Godly form;
The other side, that grooves with the subtle
Rasa of Shringaar.

Nataraj - The half and the whole,
So blunt yet coy, supple rhythms roll;
To infinity – the dance of perfect harmony.

We surrender – to him who holds time,
To the one who rules melody,
In every gesture, in every strike,

Nataraj,
The Lord of Dance,
Of rhythms infinite.

3. Guru Paran

[Taal: Ashtamangal, 11 matra, Madhya Laya]

Dhanan dhanan dha Ghen ta dha ghen ta
Dhyan dharo ||
Ghanan ghanan agyaat agyaani ka gyaan
bharo ||
Maya moh bandh taran naran traan sadho ||
Kaam krodh taj dha kraan Kradhaan karam
rajo ||
Dha terekete tete Ta terekete tete Nritya taal
sulape lahoo me tumhaar ||
Tanan tanan tum Tirwati mann mora Disha
dharo ||
Naman karun main Guru tumhari sadhana
jap tap ko ||
Sarathi ban mere sadhana rath mori raas
dharo ||

Raas dharo Guru Raas dharo
Tum Raas dharo ||
Takita dhet ta Dhum kit tak
Takit taan dha dhati dha
Dhage tete Tage tete

Ghene dhage Tete kete
Takita taan dha
Dha ti dha dha ti dha dha ti ‖
Dha X

4. An Ode to My Guru {Translated}

Dhanan dhanan dha: I pray for your voice –
To lift my heart – focus, unnoise.
Let your ancient light create the space,
Let all thoughts blend into your sacred lace.

I pray you undo all Maya and mysteries,
The unknowns, the Goth, that pry into me.
I pray you break the feeble chains of illusion,
Unwrap me, lead me to you, to freedom.

Unleash your rhythm on my humble sway.
Let your winds blow all my anger away.
I pray you help defeat my Earthly wants,
As I step deeper, into your wise commands.

Dha terekete tete, Ta terekete tete:
As Nritya flickers, in the continuum in you,
I pray you hold my pirouettes too.
Keep my mind tight under your glance,
Save me from all overwhelms, I chant!

I bow in humble awe to your practice –
Your persistence, your perseverance.
I bow to your devotion, Your path, your
essence.
In my task to spread your colossal work
My divine mystic, lend me your enlit spark.

5. Radha Aayi

[Taal: Teentaal, 16 matra, Drut Laya]

Dig dig dig dig dig dig dig dig
Radha aayi Gopi aayi ||

Dig dig dig dig aayi
Sab sakhi lekar aayi ||

Dig dig dig dig dig dig dig dig
Radha aayi Radha aayi ||

Dig dig Gopi aayi
Sau (100) sakhi sang layi ||

Sau kilkari rang layi
Umarh ghumarh ke, tann ban ke ||

Sab aayi,
Dig dig Radha aayi Radha aayi ||

Lapak jhapak ke, Bahak thahak ke,
Shaam galin Paigaam aayi ||

Hai Radha aayi
Sang sab Gopin aayi ||

Sau kilkari sang layi
Dekho Dekho Dekho Radha ||
Aayi X

6. Radha's Arrival
{Translated}

Radha arrives with her Gopi crew.
Gleeful chatter and chirps ensue.
She brings with her, her hundred pals,
Laughter, giggles, cuckles, and all.
Radha arrives with her Gopi crew.

Infinite joy, shimmering hues,
As Radha chimes by, her eyes allure.
Tip-toeing feet – all eyes enthralled,
Radha arrives, her Gopis alight.

The townsmen chime in sans much ado.
Kanha snoops in, his Gwal friends in queue.
Their toe-tips itch, keen to join her ball,
Sway as free, let their hearts take a twirl,
As Radha arrives with her Gopi crew –
A hundred songs fill up the sight.

7. Meghamay Vrindavan

[Taal: Pancham Sawari, 15 matra, Madhya
Laya]

Ghanan ghanan ghanan ghanan nana
Thirar thirar thirar thirar thirkana ||

Mor naache nache Banke Bihari
Tribhuvan Dhari
Thei ta thei ta ||

Thei thei Nache komal Rai
Thun thun thoranga
Naache mrugaai ||

Tat tat thei ta thei
Tram thei Tram thei Tra-m
Tat tat thei Tat tat thei Tat tat Thei Thei ||
Thei
X

8. Vrindavan through the Clouds {Translated}

The clouds growl as they come closer.
The sky opens into cracks of thunder.
Strikes of lightning
Send shivers and shrieks.
The peacock taps, shaking his plumes,
She watches the splendour.

Krishna flaunts his beautiful form
As he struts around creating a gleeful storm.
On his tiny finger
Rest three divine worlds.
Sri Radha twirls in grace –
Light spins, sweet steps, defying all norms.

The little fawn springs in bliss unheld,
As we chant hymns praising this holy spell.
Aum!

9. Viraha

[Taal: Basant, 9 matra, Madhya Laya]

Timir gagan, Ghana ghor -
Sab Mann tadpat ||

Nishabd nirav, Jahkjhore sab –
Sukh hai paraast ||

Ghor kaal chhav, chaaun ban Chand
Chupa lenhi ||

Jor andhiyar, swar vichalit
Chitt gambheer ||

Krishnaleen hai Krishnaheen
Vivash adheer ||

Rudit hank, Krishna naam
Nayan aneer ||

Bheed achal, abadh abal
Vikshipt vileen ||

Sudh visrai Ralarola sab
Ujad ashaleen ||

Shyaam aao, sab trast vichalit
dhoondhat tumhe ||

Hatthi agyaan, phire bhool Nij
Komal hriday ||

Phire bhool, tav Shree charan
Raje komal hriday ||

Vah hriday, jahan viraje sadaiv
Prabhu Sadanand ||

Bhoolein kaise woh sabhi tav Nirat aalingan
||
Prabhu Krishnaheen karo Krishnadheen
Punah ||

Hum murali hai sab, tum
Sadananda ||
Pravah X

10. Viraha – Wilting, Away from You {Translated}

In the haunting rhythm of nightfall,
The village hums the absence of His
presence—
A silence quivers with the echoes of longing.

Shadows gather,
Their hearts a sea of restless waves,
Murmuring in the moonlight,
Weaving sorrow and devotion into a single,
fragile thread.

Krishna has vanished,
A fleeting shadow slipping through –
Ruthless folds of reality.
As they stand in the emptiness,
A chorus of souls wail.

The voices rise,
A lament woven from the notes of yearning.

Each note – a testament to their boundless
love.
Love that they say is helpless! Stubborn.
They seek your sight.

They seek your sight.
Forgotten self. Frail, unprotected.
They speak of a love so profound,
It eclipses the stars, transcends Earth!
Dances restless - beyond the grasp of mortal
understanding!
Unfathomed depths of attachment –
Weakening every pulse.

In their song, time bends,
The boundaries of the self dissolves.
Palpable sorrow, forgotten truth –
Of where his lotus feet still rest.
Forgotten what burns unspoken within every
heart.
Forgetting to look where they can find a
reflection of you.
A glimpse of Krishna's eternal embrace,
Rests hidden within the pain, their devotion.
Their holy heart.

We are the mystical flutes
Playing your sweetest tunes of enchanting
divinity.
Every note – a celebration and a plea.
Every sigh as potent as Dhanvantari.
Healing with the profound truth.
Delivering the bliss of the One.

Reviving. Renewing. Rejuvenating. Aum.

11. Navaras – Prakriti aur Yog

[Taal: Jhaptaal, 10 matra, Madhya Laya]

Shringaar:
Bhor bhaye bhramara kilake dekh rajit kusum
saaj ||
Karat suchhand umang it ut dekh Makarand
||
Tirchhay nayan mridu haas chaahe Milind
madir Yog ||
Raas X

Hasya:
Ek ghumadta megh, dekh Raudra satej, kare
manan ||
Tum prachanda dhoop, mera rasila swaroop,
karun khandan ||
Jeun soch so thahak, hansa chabila dhanak,
thatholi ||
Vinodan X

Karuna:

Ek yug bhaye beh aayi tarangini ek ma
||
Bhar sukh chahun aur phal phool anukul
upahar ||
Phir niyati alekh dhar uchcha pravah
bheeshan ||
Ma sidhaar rahi maha sangam namm sajal
nayan ||
Hai thithurte adhar kunch bhaal ati rudita
karun ||
Mann X

Raudra:

Unmukt jalprapaat takit dhet dhet nirantar
aghat ||
Ashant uchcha naad kradhet-tan garaje
teekshnatar kataar ||
Ghen tadha tadha hai prastar pareshan aur
jalaj lahulahan ||
Dhageterekete dhaDhage tereketedha
Dhageterekete dha hai yeh Raudra nirday ati ||
Prachand X

Veer:
O he Maralo ka jhund tum shoor ho apar
durant ||
Ati tej mahaveer ho abadh sudheer, pag
pralamb ||
Kar yatra aviral chalo duur avikal sakutumb
||
Liye Suryadev ke bal tane kesariya pankh
jeete Jagat ||
Jung X

Bhayanak:
Ek ati tung parvat par buss raha vah tuchha
heembind ||
Aakar ati ksheen magar balsheel antaheen
nahi woh paradheen ||
Kabhi bhi nanha bind kar uthe akasmik gar
hulchal ||
Kar vishal himskhalan ludakte ladkhadate kar
aloran ||
Machayega vo ghor hahakar hanke tej tushar
dhaar ||
Pind ban pralay ek prachand hai sabko kar
dharasaai ||

Dekh nanha tushar kan soche bhayavah vo
kshan tan man ||
Siharan X

Vibhatsa:
Thirak sisak reng aaya ek pankil sarisrip
||
Liye shalk bhare chhaal dehmay kar roop
vikrit ||
Utha siharan chahu aur dekh woh lacheela
badan ||
Mand mand kunchit kenchuli kare udar
manthan ||
Dekh daldali drishya visri hua vichalit chitt
||
Thir-thir kaanp utha tan jab thirraya wah
kenchuli ||
Kunchit X

Adbhutah:
Hua sheet ka ant aaya rangeen bahar basant
||
Ghor nidra se jaag aaya reech kshudhit
vichalit ||

Aur hua stambhit vismit dekh maas
pushpasikt   ‖
Hai prafulla chahun-dis nit ramya raag bhor
suvarnit   ‖
Phir chakshu unmilit mandasmit chala reech
ati   ‖
Amodit X

Shanta:
Ek shubh raatri Krishna paksha hai Triyama
prahar   ‖
Ek akela sa mekh ghere chand kare ghor
andhkar   ‖
Jag nidramagn ati shant nahi koi aloran ‖
Hai Prashant Gambheer ati aviral timir yah
kshan   ‖
Nayn ardhonmilit mridu swas din kare
nimantran   ‖
Ramya yogi sthir-chitt atal-dhyaan
parabramha shant maha-   ‖
Milan X

12. Navaras Haiku: Universe in Yog {Translated}

Shringaar

[Permanent mood – Love; associated with attractiveness, beauty]

Love of bee and blooms
Sprightly rhythms shy glance lit
Smiles longing Yog

Hasya

[Permanent mood – Humor; associated with laughter due to silly acts, brazenness, sarcasm, and mockery]

A dancing nimbus
Scoffs at fuming Sun, then rains
Zany rainbow grins

Karuna

[Permanent mood – Grief; associated with
compassion, empathy, sorry]

River, Mother – bless
Fate prevails, tears bid adieu
Heaving chest - sighs doom

Raudra

[Permanent mood – Wrath; associated with
anger, fury, expressions of fits of rage]

Mammoth waterfalls
Raging stabs – bleeds water esse
Chill, shrill, remorseless.

Veer

[Permanent mood – Courage; associated with
bravery and heroism, grit and resilience]

Flaming flamingos
So fast yet stoic, blush, stretched grit
Resilience shines through

Bhayanak
[Permanent mood – Fear; associated with
terror induced by an unsettling feeling of
lurking danger/threats; hit the primal chords
of life's fragility]

Atop rests meek snow
Ghoul terror, looming avalanche
Shivers cut down spine

Vibhatsa

[Permanent mood – Disgust; associated with
responses or feeling towards repulsive things]

Squirm slithering scales
Slippery slimes my skin crawls
Queasy snake skin sheds

Adbhutah
[Permanent mood – Wonder/Awe; associated
with a sense of amazement when faced with
the extraordinary, thus reminding of the
amazing beauties that exist]

Cold recedes bear wakes
Awestruck, dazed, resplendent spring
Eyes wide, smiles alit.

Shanta
[Pernanent mood – Indifference/detachment;
it is understood that all Rasa's emerge from
and dissolve into this emotion. Shanta is
considered the only permanent emotion.]

Night wanes, souls still sleep
Eyes sublit, serene, deep – calls
Yogi absorbs bliss.

13. Shiv Paran

[Taal: Chautaal, 12 matra, Vilambit Laya]

Drig drig drig drig Dambaru baaje
Ghir ghir Shankar Swayambhu naache
Thir thir ghe ghe ghe ghe chamake Nilambar ||

Kran dha kradhet ta Tit kata gadi ghene dha
Chamake nilambar Ganga chhalotchhala
Thilanga jhijhikata Tit kata thun thun dha ||

Gati badhat Nat Nat nache Natvar
Ta Dhari kit tak Jhejhe dha
Jhejhe dha Jhejhe dha Jhe jhe ||

Chamakata Bhairava koti Chandra Prabha
Trinetra Jwala Jwala Smit-mukh Varabhay
Vishnu Prajapati Ananta stuti Rata ||

Shiv Shiv Mahadev Har Har Mahadev
Har Har Bhay
Har Har Bhay Har Har Bhay Har Har Bhay
Har Har ||

Ta dharikittaka Traan dha
Drig drig drimi drimi dhet dhet dha
Taka drig jhijhikata Taka drig jhijhikata   ‖

Dum dum dum dum jhe jhe ta thunga
Thun thun thoranga Thun thun thoranga
Mahadev nache Mahadev nache   ‖

Mahadev nache Dha Tat
Kra dhan dhan Dhati dha Kra dhan dhan
Dhati dha
Kra dhan dhan dha ti ‖
Dha
X

14. A Dance of Shiva – The Eternal One {Translated}

Drig drig drig - The damaru has begun its
strums in your gracious hands.
O' dancing Shiva, O' self-born one, O'
merciful protector,
Your blazing pirouettes create guardian rings
of fire.

The blue sky cracks a cosmic arc with every
step,
Beaming with the glow of your infinite.
As gracious Ganga shimmies down your
knotted dreadlocks,
The stars, the ethereal souls, witness your
divine dance,
Twinkling in awe.

As you surge the tempo,
Your shimmer leaves every being spellbound.
Your divine smile promising us your vigilance,

That you will destroy
All evil that befalls your devotees –
O' merciful Natavar!

As the rhythm deepens O' Bhairava,
You radiate the glow of a countless moons;
Your Trinetra ablaze with the eternal fire.
Vishnu and Prajapati are singing endless
hymns praising You,
O' endless one.

O' Mahadev, O' greatest Lord,
We pray you heal our fears.
In the cosmic rhythm, our sacred prayer
unfolds –
Infinite chants "Har Har Har"
Create an infinite echo of our calls to you
O' blissful, infinite one!

15. Hori

[Taal: Teentaal, 16 matra, Drut Laya]

Sarpat hatt chali raaj basant hori ||
Sar sar sar bhari gaun abeera ||
Chakh shehtoot SS dig dig tho dig dig tho ||
Chakh shehtoot matang phiri mouchakhi ||
Ghosla sambhal baithi chatura goraiya ||
Dhinn dhinn ta na
Na dig dig dig thei ||
tho dig dig dig thei takit dhikit thei
SS T t t thei ||

Awlakki chattkaare Madan Manohar ||
Gwal bacchda sang Radhe pukaare ||
Raadhe
Komal kar mal ||
Tesu ati bhaari Tesu ati bhaari ||
Kilak kilak shyaam sudh bisraye ||

Ta thei thei tat Aa thei thei tat
Tarikit thei tarikit thei tarikit ||
Idhar Radhe sang sakhiyan chaturiyan ||
Shyaam rang bujhh harashe ullase ||

Tapur nupur tode bandh bandh kar chip ||
Har r r r r kar Kanha thaam linhi ||

Dhumak dhinak dhin dha
Ta Dha ta Dha ta ||
Dha Dha ti dha
Chakit Kanha tab ||
Hhue dharashai
Rakt nayan jwale ||
Radhe hunkari Radha Radha ||

Ghir ghir sab sakhi rang hai daari ||
Radha na na
Ghir ghir sab sakhi ||
Rang hai daari
Tum tana na na nana ||
Radhe matiwari
Ghumad ghumad ghumm ||
Kanha ko nihari
Aa ha ||

Ta thunga ta thunga dig dig ta dig dig ta ||

26

Dig dig aa
Idhar Sudama ||

Idhar Sudama dekh Rai se minati kar ||
Komal mridu mann Rai Shyaam chodi ||

Manohar mukh Shyaam dekh Radhika ko
bole ||
Ab dekho kaise main rangu tumhe hori ||

Main rangu tumhe hori Main rangu tumhe
hori ||
Tharikit Tharikit Tharikit Dhin
Tharikit Tharikit Dhin
Tharikit Tharikit Dhin 1 2 3
Tharikit Tharikit Tharikit Dhin
Tharikit Tharikit Dhin
Tharikit Tharikit Dhin 1 2 3
Tharikit Tharikit Tharikit Dhin
Tharikit Tharikit Dhin
Tharikit Tharikit
Dhin
X

16. A Ballad of Holi Mischiefs {Translated}

Blooms of spring paint way for the color fest,
A blessed little town fills with chaste temple
whiffs.
The sunbirds chirp on sweet mulberries,
The witty sparrow guards her nesting tree.
But lo! Krishna, the thief of hearts,
Appears – slurping on a gooseberry so tart,
His eyes twinkling with mischievous glee,
For Radha's cheeks he longs to see.

Krishna, flushed in love, cheeks like crimson
dew,
Soft palms, mashed blooms, blushed fiery hue.
With laughter inside, his heart feels the race,
O' to paint his beloved's gentle face.
A playful scene appears, joy blooms,
As Basant sprays the town with its fine
perfume.

Now Radha, calm and wise, her friends astute,
Decode Kanha's plan utterly mute.
They giggle and tie their anklets tight,
Sneaking behind in the soft twilight.
Together they nab Shyam with flair,
Poor Krishna, shocked, is caught unaware.
Down he falls almost stupefied,
"Radha! Radha!"—he threatens a chide.

Radha's giggles refuse to cease.
Gopi's circle Kanha – dance and tease.
Coloring their beloved's cheeks without a care,
"Stop, Radha! Na, na!" he cries in despair.
The dance of love and playful spree,
Melt hearts, heal, and unite in ecstasy.

Sudama, dear friend, comes rushing to rescue,
Pleads to Radha, her heart soft as dew.
Merciful Radha, with a smile so kind,
Releases Kanha from her Gopis' tide.
Poor Krishna, flushed cheeks, crushed pride,
Warns Raai, Holi has not quite arrived.

As Krishna plans to recover his fallen Holi
fight,
Precious Radha still chuckling in sweet
delight,
Basks at the mischief they've pulled off
tonight.
And Bhaktas, with hearts in faithful flurry,
Rejoice in the divine Raas Leela of Glory.
Smearing each other with sheer love at Holi!

17. Desh Paran – Bharat

[Taal: Rupak, 7 matra, Drut Laya]

Dhagine dhage tete || Tagine tage tete ||
Dhagine dhage tete || Tagine tage tete ||

Jayati jai jai || Maatri bhumi ||
Har lahu me || Bahe tumhi ||
Snigdha sheetal || Kanak kanan ||
Tapta Kanchan || Chaav tumhari ||
Dhagine dhete dhete || Madhur kanti ||
Tagine tete tete || Janani nyaari ||

Uttare Shiv || Damru dhyayein ||
Jat me ulajhe || Ganga nyaari ||
Brahmaputra || Ganga dhaayein ||
Vaam bhuj raje || Saat Saheli ||
Dhadhin thun ga na || Ta dhin thun ga na ||
Tin tir kit ta || Tir kit tit tir kit tit tit ||

Sarasa Mahanadi || Tapi Narmada ||
Saje hain tumpe || Jaise Mekhala ||
Krishna Kauvery || Tungabhadra ||
Nirat sadhte hain || Trigun tumhri ||

Pagme sajte hai || Anant Periyar ||
Ti ti na dhi na dhi na || Madhur Shinjini ||

Dahin anshe || Ajeya Shiv dhuni ||
Dig dig dig dug dug dig dig || Taraan dha ||
Dahin anshe ajeya || Shiv dhuni ||
Harashe kilakata || Sabarmati ||

Kradhinn thunga || ghinna ghin nana ||
Ta --- || Ghir nak dhit dhit ||

Ananta antare || Sada virajata ||
Akhanda avirat || Bhaav jyoti ||
Aseem anahat || Apar – abaadh ||
Prashanti || Dhinn dhinn nana ||
Dhinn dhinn nana || Dhinn dhinn nana ||
Dha
X

18. An Ode to My Motherland {Translated}

I chant a million praises in your Glory –
My radiant motherland.
Your brilliant glow tides
And your shimmering silence calms
Through my devout bloodstrands.

I chant a million praises in your Glory –
My mystical roots harnessed.
You reminisce on Shiva's mystic notes.
The healing waters bless,
My seven sisters caress.

I chant a million praises in your Glory –
Your chants cleanse my tongue.
The ripples on you dazzling drapes,
So many gorgeous trinkets strung.
Our lives enbliss upswung!

So, we chant a million praises in your Glory –
O' unique Bharat desh.
We bow in humble grace,

As we stand on your heritage.
Humbled, blessed, amazed!

Section 2: The Spirit and Dance of Kathak Yog

"Poetry is when an emotion has found its
thoughts and the thought has found its words."
						~ Robert Frost

In this section we unleash a Kathak Dancer's
Journey to the Spirit.
Aum!

..

1. KathakYog Prayer to Every Beginning

Your urja travels to me. I am blessed.
Energies sublime. Divine Sun and Moon.
Tide n' ebb sway each breath, at your behest.

My prana flows in, pulsing in my chest.
It flows, it zens, it bliss, it cleanse. I bloom.
Your urja travels to me. I am blessed.

Connecting all – be it Earth, or fire intense,
Or flowing water, or calm of air. I swoon.
Tide n' ebb - each breath at your behest.

I climb, the toil, Climax. The drain. I rest.
Attain ethereal bliss. Solitaire. A boon.
Your urja has travelled to me. I am blessed.

At last clamouring to the void. You rest.
Behold. A sweet unfathomed lagoon.
Tide n' ebb sway each breath, at your behest.

Then it stops. The Yogi is all that's left.

The sweet, the sweat, the void, the You.
Your urja travels to me. I am blessed.
Tide n' ebb sway each breath, at your behest.

2. Axioms of Faith

My faith resounds with every strike of taal,
A sweet prayer is sent.
My faith reverbs with every beat that goes amiss,
A lesson finds new strength.
My faith sweetens with every spin, each frill, each
twirl,
A speck is released with your essence.
My faith blooms with every arc the arm draws,
Imagination soars high on raw wings.
My faith twinkles with every sway of the eyes,
Silver sprinkles down where the sky ends.
My faith ignites with every dance that sings your
grace,
You hum through in every stance.
My faith stays in peace for even on the darkest
days,
Your lamp stays aglow, a sparkle ascends.

You are the storyteller. You are Yog. You are divine
dance.
The universe bears testament.

3. The Kathak's Dance of Eternal Panchakritya

In the Kathak's body, eternal energies create an
epiphany,
Aligned to ignite energy rhythms synced to the
universal timbre.
As affluent as the timeless cosmic meter.
Five sacred forces chorus, chime in the perfect
symphony.

Srishti breathes melodies of life, accompanying
the Kathak
Through a divine trance. Creations appear.
Endless forms, infinite visions. Games of "Upaj"
allure -
Stringed layakari, improvised padhant,
enamouring Gat.

Sthiti holds the decorum, with grace so wise.
Utpatti transpires to Thaat. Gracing each strike of
Sam – the first.
Preserving, steady pulse through each riyaaz, every
strut.
Grace, rhythm, poise - adhere as tamed allies.

Samhara of the Paran. Deconstructing multitudes
of complexities.
Fierce. Magnificent.
Veer notes. Portent.
Paran – echoes of the absolute truth with cryptic
rhapsodies.

Tirobhava veils the astute identity.
Tapping hard Tatkaar.
Muffling ego, delusions of unaware.
Taming ignorance. Emphasizing on truth of
non-duality.

At last, Anugraha – everlasting blessings.
Assurance.
Mirrored in Uthaan, towards the start. Lifted
energy. Soaring spirit.
Simple sounds reminding of the ultimate mystic.
Rhythms of grace. Raised to seek the divine
glance.

Thus, cruising through a journey of magnificence.
Enraptured in divine fables of the one who's the
sweetest.
A Kathak's heart unfolds to create, to share, in
praise.
Tales of truth, Karma, Surrender, Balance.

4. Dawn

Feet land on the cold tiles
A few sips to appease parched throat.
What dreams! Calm down O sweet new day.
Cradle in to a new beginning -
Songbirds have begun announcing the arrival,
The returning rays are still a while away.
Stretch, lift, reach up.
Touch those feet that hold, carry.
Peep in – a pair of wings, a fay!
Peace be on all souls.
Ground still cold from the night.
Yet healed and steady to hold a pray.
A lamp lights up, flowers awake -
Incense all around breathing in new energy.
Silence. Sombre. A sprightly blue jay.
Breath sways, chants welcome in
The returning rays as they land between the eyes
Rekindling spirits, body, the way.
Crystal drops start shimmering on the face,
Hands join in prayer grateful for another go.
Another push, another spell of bliss.
Another chance to burnish the clay.

5. Guru - My ephemeral Guide

I see your radiance in both your worldly and
transcendental states –
Blinding and soothing at the same time.
I see the sheen of the Moon and the fire of the
Sun in you.
You are the pure scent of Earth.
Your words fall into my ears like the first whisper
of Vedas,
Echoing AUM as you speak to me.
Your hand on my head feels like a dip in holy
Ganga –
Healing me, making me bloom again.
You are the taste in Rasa after an immaculate
recital.
You are the fruit of my Sadhana.
You are the seed for my creative sparks.
Let your brilliance shine through me as Seva.
O precious Guru, hold my hand always, guiding
me to the light of your work.

6. Advaitaha - Non-dual

Is it the way of Narcissus -
To know that I am you?
Or is it humbling - to look around,
Realize every other being is too?

To believe that the cradle in which I lay every
minute
Is rested and cajoled to inspire;
Is protected and nurtured
In realms where self and cosmos intertwine.
Advait. Non-dual. Your grand method unfolds.

To envision this truth – the humble heart has to
resign;
Yet claim the soul's dominion, fierce and bold.
Advait: You and I – inseparable, one.
Proud, humbled. Sweat drops tremble down -
Screaming - "Hail You, My Lord".

In the haze, the ego fades away.
Fuzzy shadows yield to light's unblemished grace.
Seeing the self as merely part of whole, yet
complete.
Boundaries dissolve in a cosmic dance.

Advait. Non-dual. Wisdom's lofty goal.
Or craft the guise of self-importance' prance.
In humble heart or vanity's embrace,
Your marvellous truth collected in stance.

7. Swadhyaya -
Reflections on Self

Can I see me? As I dance?
Can I hear me recite? My own Padhant?
Can I feel my emotions?
Drink the rasa that flows?

They say - I have never seen my own face
As everyone else sees mine.
Or hear my own melody like you do
When I sing to you.

Not with my worldly senses. I am sure.
The me that you see – the outer sheath?
The I – protected within
My own silk cocoon.

I can see me when I dance – to my own Padhant.
I hear my own divine melody;
I can feel the rasa that you feel through my dance,
When I take a few steps into the truth that resides
in me.
I see, I hear, I feel, as you do,
When I dance to you!

8. Sarasvati - The Divine Mother, the Muse, the Enchantress

Moonlit blossoms, ivory sandal paste,
Silk drapes bloom with radiance chaste,
White pearls adorn – hair, neck, ears,
White conchshells, croon melodies in your praise.
Devi, you are worshipped in Vedas in countless
ways.

I fathom the dewy curve of the bow on your lips,
Smiling in grace you retain purity of spirits.
Your shine exceeds that of many million moons.
You are devoid of gloom, scars, malice.
Devi, you are worshipped by the Trinity excelsis.

You hold the ancient wisdom in your divine
hands.
Devi, you erase all anomalies from the holy
chants.
You are the epitome of grace, of Vidya infinite.
You hold the conscious strings of cosmic dance.
Devi, you hold the supreme intellect in your
trance.

Your Veena weaves melodies that cajole the
universe.
Devi, you keep the planets in union singing your
praise.
You dance in grace atip the tongues of pundits.
Devi, you are the muse, you rule all creative
prowess.
O' Matangi you are the cosmic force the essence
of all Ras.

You are the sky and you are the nest.
You shine through Vedic chants, in hearts of yogis
- You rest.
You're not merely an embodiment of the Tridevi,
Tantra shakti thrives on your infinite zest.
Devi, you sow creative tryst, garner art flow, reap
excellence.

You are the holy mother flowing as the ancient
river.
You are fertility; your Purity transcending mere
water.
You sow the essence of piety in mere beings.
You reside on the intellect of the devout reader.
Devi you hold the light, you guide, you conquer.

You harp on cosmic energies create brilliance.
Of profound intellect, You are the core essence.
You keep Parabrahm intoxicated with your
infinite wisdom.
Krishna hums divine tunes to your grace.
Mahadev sways in bliss, adoring your divine haze.

O divine Mother, O muse of artistic spree –
Make me your white lotus, or unwavered swan,
or your citramekhala, may be;
Let my art transcend through your palette of
grandeur,
And weave yarns of your splendid will, your
divine decree.
O' mesmerising Matangi, divine mother Sarasvati,
Pray you shine your brilliance through me.

9. Surya Namaskar - The Holy Union

Hands join at the heart in grace
Eyes close searching you in the centre of all
Arms raise in prayer touching your lotus feet
Stretching open the heart for them to rest on.
Then engulfing those precious feet in
Towering self down to touch my own.
We are one.
You stretch and pull back the reigns on me
Guiding me as the rider on their horse
You give me strength to support divine energy
I kiss your lotus feet again,
Feet, knees, chest, palms, chin bowed humbly in
your grace.
You make me rise again, like the serpent,
Opening out the heart, the breath, the voice.
Bow again like the mountains at your feet,
When you ride again my reigns taut in your holy
hold
I touch my feet after the holy bath once more.
You make me rise, resting your feet on my heart,
As I swing my head back to make you a seat again.
I bow in Pranam. Grace be to you, my Lord.

10. An Ode to Dance

The feet begin with the tap and the dhin,
Striking an energy enough to cast a million spells.
Hips shift with the gait and waves whirl up from
the frolicking legs.
The waist sways, tuning in to the storm arising
from below.
Chest curls and grooves, teaming up with
perfectly sliding shoulders.
Arms rise, draw splendid forms, roll magic down
through slender fingers.
Neck connects to the hips again, rolling and
shifting as she turns.
The lips curl.
The nose twitches.
Eyes follow the fingers throughout, weaving
stories of the heavens.
Brows curve up and curl, adding subtly to the
magic of divine Rasa.
Hair stays taut, lest it interrupts the beauty of
rhythm.
The head rests in eternal solace, through all.

11. An Ode to Feet

Have you seen my feet?
Focus on them when I dance.
Did they just miss a beat?
Did you skip one?
Did you think they need another swipe on the
whet stone?

When you saw those feet,
Did you see where they've walked through?
All the smiles, tears, and sweat;
A few dreams dreamt, a few lived;
A few crushed, a few new weaved.

My feet can tell you stories –
Of mine, my Gods, my demons.
They can wince in pain and smile as well.
They can curl in bliss and unfold again.
They can paint, where you would fill the words.
They can pep up fables mundane.

Did you see your feet today?
Did you pamper them last night?
They hold your courage, calm, and grace,
You anger, frustrations, and plight;
Your values, your darkness, and your light.

Strung in gold bells, my feet strike tunes;
They tap, they beat, and they prance;
They strut, they brag, atone when amiss;
They string – unstring, they dance.

12. The Ghungroos

In twilight's hush, each breath holds still in grace,
Gold drops entwine her ankles, muffled chimes,
Her ghungroos twirl and tap with silver threads.
As cymbals ring as soft as moon's embrace,
A goldfinch croons a tune to sync her time.
In twilight's hush, their breaths hold still in grace.

Their symphony plucks at stars as if to tease,
Each bell a note of celestial awe aligned,
Her ghungroos twirl and tap with silver threads.

Through fields of time, unfold eternal steps,
In every turn, a tale of grace unwinds,
In twilight's hush, her breath holds still in grace

A watching moon, a journey bright beneath.
Through form to heart, the dancer's act refines,
Her ghungroos twirl and tap with silver threads.

Her feet, like whispers, glide where spirits tread,
From earthly bounds to harbors of divine,
In twilight's hush, her breath holds still in grace
Her ghungroos twirl and tap with silver threads.

13. Anandohum – I am Bliss

I dance. I am bliss.
My dance transcends to the infinite, seeks
freedom, seeks joy.
Its nature refuses to be obscured by that act,
Which is done by the compulsion of want or fear.
It does not seek freedom from action.
My blissful dance seeks freedom in action.

My dance is love, lost in the light of the moon.
My dance is grace, lost in the lustre of Shiv.
My dance is your touch, lost in a longing to sway
to your rhythm.
My dance is devotion, lost in the afterglow of your
name.
My dance is today, lost in the reverberations of
time.

My dance is You. I am in bliss.
I dance. I am Sadashiv.

14. Swaramaya – A Day tuned into the Ragas

Eyes open in the quiet. Sleep still shrouds surroundings.
Alone. Without a need.
Enraptured by the stillness.
Enthralled by the dominant Shiv.
I hear the seven notes of **"Bhatiyar"**.
Ma Ganga bathing my spirit with her grace.

Humbled. My hungry mind tamed, solemn.
Voice muffles Aum, strumming seven strings of **"Bhairav"**.
Breathing in the magnificence of my Lord.
Grounding with the energies of the Mother.
My fragrant breath resounds **"Lalit"**. Alive.
Longing for the joys that rest within.

Hums and whistles, I stroll through a lofty day
A little bird chimes in – I name him **"Bilawal"**.
His joyful chirps weave into mine. Together we chant **"Bhairavi"**.
Stirring up a melody inspired by awe – to the beauty that surrounds.

The Sun fires up, reminding us of the duties that
lay strewn.
Commanding in the decibels of "Deskar". Fiercely
nudging to complete what I've begun.
I settle into a devoted state of flow;
dissolving the endless knots of chores with the
lithe "**Dev Gandhar**".

Accomplished a tall order; I gently sway back to
rest.
Soaked in the fruitfulness of a beautiful day
waning.
"**Shudh Sarang**" lays a lush drape on me.
Lulling me to the sweetest siesta.

Was that too long? So much to do still!

The evening sets in with old friends "**Pilu**" and
"**Marwa**".
We sulk together, regretting lost time.
Lost gains. Lost moments.
Our deep sighs deepen the air.
The lamp stands still.

My Lord steps in again.
"**Nat Bhairav**".
Realizing the beauty of the wealth that lies
untold.

Head bowed in shame; remorse steps aside.
A gentle breeze floats in **"Bahaar"**. Making room
for the subtle realization.
I look at what is already mine. Grace.

The day wraps up, counting blessings.
I lean in to **"Hamir"**. He has just announced the
approaching new day.
I plan. Then - I hum Aum. Soothing with **"Kedar"**.
Staring into the countless blessings that shine at
me from Him.
Eyelids droop, heavy with grace.
My bliss body sinks to the groove.
The gravity of it nudges me onto your **"Darbaar"**.
I surrender to your tuneful intentions.
The tapestry of surmay Ragas, weaving up each
blessed day.
Tuning our melody to You.

15. A Mystic's unsung musings on Ashtanayika

In the garden of the soul,
eight heroines bloom,
each a facet of the travelling heart,
each a mirror to the Yogi's path.

Swadhinbhartruka - The Powerful One
[She is radiant with contentment and control in
her relationship - with her only true love]

In the quiet dawn,
she breathes in the sacred stillness.
Each asana – a brushstroke
on the canvas of her being.
Resolute contentment weaving through her veins.

Her persona – confident, pleased;
Her heart – a lotus unfurling;
Poised with unwavered discipline, practice.
Roots run deep all the way in.
Grounded to her Self.

She dances with her shadow,
in sacred union of self and spirit;

each pose – a testament to her Master.

She is a shimmering sunbeam,
Radiating through her sadhana.
Content in her solitude – in unmistaken union
with the One,
the universe wraps around her spirit – like a warm
shawl.

Vasakasajja - The One who is ready
[She has decorated herself to receive her loved
one. She is excited and ready for union]

Draped in faith,
She adorns herself with intentions.
Each embellishment holding a promise,
Every thread of her attire whispering a prayer.
A flicker of hope rests aflame,
fluttering in the depths of her chest.

She stands on the precipice of connection,
She prepares her heart as a temple,
Her craft is her ritual,
Her art – a sacred Sadhana.

A bridge spans the chasm of longing,
With each passing moment.

She readies herself to dissolve,
In eternal bliss of the divine embrace.

Virahakhandita / Utkanthita - The Distressed One
[She has been away from her loved one and is
waiting for him, anxious to meet]

Her forlorn heart sulks – grim with the absence:
each breath a resounding lament,
for the placid bliss of sadhana has been slipping
through her fingers.

Days leave shadows in its wake, stretching;
Unable to arise and show up for herself.
The joy of practice a distant melody now,
anguish pouring from her lips.

The ache of separation claws into her sullen spirit.
She wails to the heavens,
"Where is my beloved?"
Her tears, like murky swollen rivers –
Carry the weight of the long separation.

Each breath bears a reminder to the distance, the
ache.
She yearns for the embrace of stillness –
that only her sweet Lord can provide.

Khandita - The Upset One
[She is angry with her lover for being unfaithful.
She scoffs at him, hiding her own inner pain.]

Her faith is frayed at the edges.
Angry words fall like stones.
She scoffs at the void,
Her heart a tempest;
Yet behind the fury,
A flicker of hurt nests.

The longing for union lays masked
By the bitterness of betrayal.
Fury rises like smoke,
Twisting and spitting at the air around her.

She lashes out –
Her calling mirrors the tryst of this rendezvous.
In her rage,
she curses the path,
the very essence of her Sadhana.
She mocks her divine with every word.

Yet beneath the storm,
A flicker of longing lingers.
Yearning solace in the madness,
Searching for the thread that ties her to her
dearest.

Abhisandhita / Kalahantarita – The remorseful one
[One separated by quarrel. Now regretful of her lost love]

Lost in the chaos of her outburst,
She realizes the depth of her solitude.
She calls out to the silence.

The echoes of her anger
Still rippling through the stillness,
Regrets the void she created.

And in that regret that has unfurled its dark wings,
Lurks a resounding yearn to return –
To embrace the calm again.

Thus, in her own - the aftermath of battle lingers,
Her heart – now a tangled vine,
Remorse coiling around her like mist. She remembers the void.

She reaches out to the emptiness.
Delving deeper into it.
Fumbling to resume her quest for the light, her love.

She is now a Yogi in contemplation.
She navigates the maze of her emotions.
Striving to return to the calm that she once knew,
Where union stood eternal.

Vipralabdha - the Deceived/ deprived One
[She is frustrated with her loved one, as she has
waited all night, but he never came. She feels
betrayed, abandoned, sad, and angry.]

The universe seems to be ignoring her calls –
Deceiving her of her dues;
Her spirit a storm of bitterness.
The faith she once held,
now crumbling like autumn leaves.
Illness curls around her,
like a fog that obscures the path.
Her heart heavy with disbelief,
As the mystic colors of Yog –
fade to gray.
Bitterness seeps into her veins.
Her skills – once vibrant,
now dull as a fading star.
She feels the weight of deception,
the cruel irony of potential unfulfilled;
Anger coils in her belly,
draining the radiance from her forehead, the flush
from her cheeks.

Each breath is a struggle,
each thought a heavy stone.
In her despair,
she seeks the light
that once had lit her path.

Proshitabhartruka - The One who is missing her
dear one
[She is missing her lover, who has gone on a trip.
She is sad due to the temporary separation.]

Her heart a vessel of longing,
battered by the winds of separation.
Each moment stretches,
an eternity without the one who is her divine.

Her faith falters like a dimming star.
She craves the light of union,
The warmth of devotion,
to awaken once more,
to rise as the Yogini she's always yearned to be.

Longing wraps around her like a shroud.
The ache of separation
sinks deep into her bones.
Days blur into one another,
the mundane eclipsing the sacred.

14. Swaramaya – A Day tuned into the Ragas

Eyes open in the quiet. Sleep still shrouds surroundings.
Alone. Without a need.
Enraptured by the stillness.
Enthralled by the dominant Shiv.
I hear the seven notes of **"Bhatiyar"**.
Ma Ganga bathing my spirit with her grace.

Humbled. My hungry mind tamed, solemn.
Voice muffles Aum, strumming seven strings of **"Bhairav"**.
Breathing in the magnificence of my Lord.
Grounding with the energies of the Mother.
My fragrant breath resounds **"Lalit"**. Alive.
Longing for the joys that rest within.

Hums and whistles, I stroll through a lofty day
A little bird chimes in – I name him **"Bilawal"**.
His joyful chirps weave into mine. Together we chant **"Bhairavi"**.
Stirring up a melody inspired by awe – to the beauty that surrounds.

The Sun fires up, reminding us of the duties that
lay strewn.
Commanding in the decibels of "**Deskar**". Fiercely
nudging to complete what I've begun.
I settle into a devoted state of flow;
dissolving the endless knots of chores with the
lithe "**Dev Gandhar**".

Accomplished a tall order; I gently sway back to
rest.
Soaked in the fruitfulness of a beautiful day
waning.
"**Shudh Sarang**" lays a lush drape on me.
Lulling me to the sweetest siesta.

Was that too long? So much to do still!

The evening sets in with old friends "**Pilu**" and
"**Marwa**".
We sulk together, regretting lost time.
Lost gains. Lost moments.
Our deep sighs deepen the air.
The lamp stands still.

My Lord steps in again.
"**Nat Bhairav**".
Realizing the beauty of the wealth that lies
untold.

She mourns the loss of devotion;
A soul adrift, unanchored in faith.
All that remains is the whisper of his name,
A beacon of her desolation.
In that space, she craves Yog again.

Abhisarika - the Courageous One
[She is very bold and has no qualms in going in
search of her love. She is smart, witty, unshaken
and pursues her love relentlessly.]

She embarks on the quest –
her spirit a wildfire that lights her path ahead.
With each step a declaration – "I will not rest
until I find you."

She dances through the shadows –
each step a celebration of intention, her grit a
compass.
And with every step she surges ahead – relentless
in pursuit.

She reflects the fearless Yogi –
following the light. Her wits sharp as mountain
air,
her joy infectious as spring blossoms. Nature en
sync, attuned.

Her journey moulds into a sacred odyssey –
every moment is like meditation, each turn is a
lesson in love.
She dances carefree; her quest alive, pure, aligned
to truth.

The Wrap:
The eight scenes of the nayika,
eight enamouring moods, a bouquet –
Peeks a journey through the soul,
echoing the path of the resolute Yogi.
Each emotion a chapter in the epic journey;
toward the ultimate union, where the heart finds
its home,
and the spirit soars free, in peace, bliss, harmony.

16. Celestial Rhythms: Shiva and Parvati's Nritya of the Elements

A scene lays adrift on the primal theatre of the
cosmos,
Shiv and Parvati step into the boundless stage,
The universe strums Aum - its first hymn.

Shiv, the Lord of Tandav,
Whirls in a tempestuous blaze,
A cosmic Bhramari of chaos and creation.
His Tatkaar creates the heartbeat of the universe,
Each tap – a crack of thunder,
Each Chari – a flash of lightning across the sky.
A river of molten stars cascade through the void.

Parvati, the quintessence of grace,
answers with her delicate Lasya,
Her movements - like gentle breeze,
Caress the ancient trees.
A shimmering Chhand upon the tranquil waters,
where lotus blossoms open in awe.

Their dance is an eternal dialogue.
And, in the silence between their steps,
the Earth listens,
the mountains sway,
the rivers pause,
and the sky holds its breath,
watching the dance of divine unity.

The firm truth of the universe bows to the fluid
grace of creativity.
Like a petal falling from an effervescent bloom.

In the divine ballet of precision and artistry.
She hums –
A melody now memorized by the Earth.
They hum –
The everlasting whisper of the divine.

17. Vishwaroopam

I have seen your Vishwaroopam.
The endlessness.
The beginnings, the ends.
The continuum of every entity.

O' Krishna, in your divine form,
A boundless expanse unfolds
An alchemy of awe and wonder.
Faces, on every side, merge and multiply;
Countless eyes, mouths, bellies, arms—
A boundless array of presence.
A million strands of hair,
Some ruthless in Raudra,
Some gracefully asway in Shringar.

You embody an Infinite vision.
The beginning that never ends,
The middle that binds everything,
The end that transcends understanding.
Your weapons and armour gleam
With the veracity of divine truth.
You rule the space between Heaven and Earth.
You are the supreme deity ruling all directions.
Your fanged mouth cradles energy to blaze the
whole Universe.

Your crown is ablaze with jewels.
Celestial garlands adorn your cosmic frame.
The divine scents of creation –
Waft through the Universe,
Woven into the fabric of your being.
In you, all of Brahman lays converged.
Brahma on his lotus,
Sages in silent reverence,
Celestial serpents coiling in awe.

You are the constant source.
Every being stems from your majestic self.
Every being is entering your divine form;
Some trembling in fear – as they are engulfed
amid Your fangs,
Some trembling in bliss – rejoicing in melodies of
Your praise.
O' Hrishikesh, in your gracious presence,
Each soul, is drawn into the vortex of your
majesty –
Seeking the bliss that lies in You.

O' merciful one, You are the unchanging truth!
You are the guardian of Dharma.
You embody the massive beaming energy
That outshines the brilliance of many million
Suns.

In humble grace I behold –
The boundless forms of your grace sublime.
The formlessness of your supremacy bestowed to
every kind.
Your endless splendor over space and time.

 In awe of You, O' Krishna, the supreme truth I
did find.
 To You, O' merciful one, our souls lay entwined.

18. From Sam to Sam

We are dancers – we hum to the Sam.
We create, we twirl, then swirl back to Sam.
Sam – the equalizer, the first one and the last.
We echo in loop, no matter where we had begun.

How far, or how close, how little, or how huge,
Sam is the goal, despite where we've begun.
Destiny heralds, Sam marks the final refuge.
We are dancers – at Sam we return.

Sam is where we find solace.
Sam is where we feel bliss too.
Sam is where we set the goal,
Be it fast or one that's slow.

We're all on the same journey, so states Sam.
A few almost there, a few just begun.
A few prancing in the middle,
That counts too!
Sam is God's mark,
We bow every time we go through.
We are dancers – we sublime at the divine Sam.

19. Children of Adi Shakti – A Ballad

Children - pure beings, pure sparks of the divine!
Just released from realms of truth. Unedited.
Untouched by the grim, sombre weight of time
Born from sacred dance of the infinite
Their tiny fists still holding sparkly stardust.
Unlearned, unassuming, new attire.
As free, as brave, as crisp, as dawn's first light,
Prancing into His universe's solemn order.

Existence begins to paint on their bare minds,
Eager to sense, build intellect, tap to our light,
Every step – discovery, every laugh divine.
Questions whirl, sashaying to possibilities untied.
Knowledge maps like galaxies ready to collide.
Symphony of innocent chaos, giggles, whimpers,
They tumble into our sphere. Unchoreographed,
Spinning His universe's solemn order.

They carry Ma's superpowers, her Holy shrine.
Their tiny hands can revise the cosmic script.
Their soft feet can dance into maps undefined.
Their energy unabashed, uncontained, untapped,
Prancing on the cusp of possibilities unlimited.

Often an empty gaze, a wise smile – they meditate,
Brave and kind, sweet with a blazing fire.
They can pirouette into His universe's quiet order.

Their gentle touch can heal wounds of time's tempest,
They are children of Nataraj and Adi Mother.
Empowered, they have begun their divine quest,
They can stir up the universe's quiet order.

20. Your Void amid Noise

Charting through the worldly whims -
Making way for every plan,
Detangling the macro, entangling some more,
I create a tiny void of You.
Demands and answers, rituals and more,
Encircled, entwined, attempting to squeeze and
shrink -
My space, my precious void of You, my lord.
I hold you still, knowing every moment
I rest safe in your cozy womb -
Nourished and cradled in peace and love.
Aum Peace!

21. Ardhanarishwar and I

Nataraj. Father. My source of all.
The energies that you bestow loads me to full
charge.
There is a glow that I feel trickle –
Spread around with my sweat.
As I spin, as I tap, as I read my bandish in one
breath.

You're the mother. The source again.
The love, the grace, the Shringaar.
The shimmer on my skin, as I sway and align.
Every angle of my body to your rhythms divine.

The cymbals on my feet create melodies of Bliss.
My skin trembles and coils.
I feel the resplendent you in my hair.
All nondivinity drops down below.
To my feet and beyond.
The breath, the sweat, the heat, the void,
confound.

I am You, oh beautiful lord!
I am Ardhanarishwar, Adiyogi.
I am the source.
I am Aum!

Section 3: Glossary

1. A Glimpse into the Kathak Yog Glossary

Adi: The first.

    Adi Shakti: [Adi – the first, Shakti – energy] The Mother Goddess who is the source of all creation.

    Adi Yogi: [Adi – the first, Yogi – ascetic] The first seeker, explorer, practitioner.

Advait: Non-dual; inseparable; One. The Advayataraka Upanishad is dedicated to elaborate on this idea of Oneness. It is one of the most important Yog Upanishads and belongs to the Shukla Yajurveda, and is dedicated to teaching how to cross over (Taraka) this concept of One soul (Advaya).

Anandohum: I am bliss

Ardhanarishwar: [Ardh – half, nari – feminine energy, woman, Ishwar – God] Ardhanarishwar is the God who adorns the form of both Shiv and Parvati, signifying the balance of truth and illusion / absolute and creation / masculine and feminine energies.

Ashtanayika: The eight heroines.

Each character has been described in poem #15, as described in Chapter 24 "Samabhinaya", of Natya Shastra by Bharat Muni.

Aum (also Om): The sound of the Universe. The sound of creation. The sound of Divine Lord.

Bandish: A composition using traditional words, syllables, rhythms, and melodies.

Bhramari: Spin or pirouette according to Natya Shastra. It is a powerful and controlled movement that can be executed only by skilled dancers. There are various types of Bhramari. In Kathak, Bhramari is more popularly known by the term "**Chakkar**".

Bramha: He is the creator God and one of the Tridevas (Trinity), along with Vishnu and Shiv.

Cari (also, **Chari**): In the Natya Shastra, Chari implies the dynamic movements of the lower body, especially one leg at a time. The feet, shanks, thighs, and hips are involved in the generally swift movements of the Cari.

Chhand: Chhand is a rhythmic element in Kathak, where improvised footwork is showcased to twist and play with Laya (tempo or speed).

Citramekhala: The divine peacock, who is also seen with Goddess Sarasvati.

Dharma: Righteousness. Right conduct. That which supports maintenance of life.

Elements: Basics. The five elements that constitute the basic building blocks of every entity are – air, water, fire, earth, and space.

Ganga: A river from Northern India, associated with divine healing powers of the Mother. She is seen studded above the left forehead of Shiv, and is also associated with other prominent deities like Devi Sarasvati.

Gat: Gait. In Kathak, Gat is performed to highlight graceful styles of the walk. Gat can be "**seedhi gat**" – graceful walks, "**gat nikas**" – where a prop like flute, water pot, peacock, snake, etc. are showcased with a complementing walk, and "**gat bhav**" – where a popular folklore from purans or religious epics is shown as a skit with abhinaya alone; i.e., without using words.

Ghungroo: Brass or silver bells tied into long cotton threads. It is a must for an Indian classical dancer to wear a pair of ghungroos around their ankles while dancing. Each side of a pair can hold 50 to 200 bells, depending on the capacity of the dancer. In general, Kathak dancers wear heavier ghungroos (more bell counts), than other classical dancers.

Guru: [Gu – darkness; Ru – one who removes] Verse 16 of the Advayataraka Upanishad sates

"**Gu** shabdastva andhakarah syat **Ru** shabdastva nirodhakah

Andhakara nirodhitvat guru rityabhidhiyate"

This simple verse explains who the Guru is to us. A Guru dispels the darkness of ignorance, thus leading us to the ultimate truth.

Hrishikesh: The Lord or controller of the mind and senses. In poem#17 Shree Krishna is addressed as "Hrishikesh", in the context of Chapter 11 of Bhagavad Gita, where the Lord has revealed his true form to Arjuna. We experience it through Sanjay's divine sight narrated to Dhritarashtra and captured in the Bhagavad Gita.

Karma: Action. Also, the accumulated fruit of past action. When, Karma is performed with integrity, without attachment, without expecting fruits of the actions being performed, and as an offering to the divine Lord, it becomes **Karma Yog**.

Krishna: The dark one. Krishna is the eighth avatar of Lord Vishnu – arrived in the Dvapar Yug to instil values of love, compassion, oneness, surrender, and Dharma.

Lasya: see **Tandav**

Layakari: Laya – tempo or speed. Layakari is a fundamental practice technique involving rhythmic variations to make exciting taal (see **Taal**) patterns. It can involve changing the division of beats (matras), or varying the speed and/or accents, thus creating intricate and captivating rhythmic patterns.

Lotus: The significance of this flower creates a beautiful highlight in Hindu scriptures that focus on Yog. Lotus is generally seen flourishing as pristine pink or white in murky and shallow water bodies. This quality signifies detachment, while staying pure and deeply rooted to its source. The long hollow stalk stays connected to the deep roots at base even while the flower floats freely with the waves and ripples. This signifies a constant state of union and bliss (see **Yog**).

Mahadev: see **Shiv**

Matangi: see **Sarasvati**

Narcissus: He is a character signifying extreme self-obsession or vanity in Greek mythology. Narcissus was the son of a River God and nymph and was admired by all for his ample beauty. Once, he saw his own reflection in the waters of a spring. He fell in love with his own image, and while seeking more of himself, he drowned.

Nataraj: The Lord of Dance. Nataraj is a dancing form of Lord Shiv, where he is seen standing with his right foot on the demon Apasmara, who signifies ego, illusion, ignorance. The Lord is performing Anand Tandav (a strong masculine dance of bliss – see **Tandav** for more details). His left leg has swayed up creating a beautiful posture showing his cosmic dance. He plays the Damaru (a small drum) with his upper right hand. He plays the sounds of creation with his Damaru, while in his upper left hand he holds Agni (fire). This and

the ring of cosmic fire that surrounds his statue
signifies his energies of creation and destruction.
In his lower right hand, he holds the Abhaya
(fearless) mudra, assuring that he will protect us
from all evil. His form is mounted on a lotus
signifying purity of all souls.

Navaras (also, Ras/ Rasa): The effect created by
the display of nine emotions. Accredited to
Bharat Muni's Natya Shastra and works of
Abhinavgupta, the Navaras depicts the nine states
of emotion. In brief - **Shringar** (love/attraction),
Hasya (laughter/humor), **Karuna**
(sorrow/compassion), **Raudra** (anger/rage), **Veer**
(heroism/courage), **Bhayanak** (terror/fright),
Bibhatsya (disgust), **Adbhuta** (surprise/wonder),
and **Shanta** (peace).

Nritya: According to Natya Shastra, dance can be
broadly categorized into two types – the **Nrtta**
and **Nritya**. Nrtta is a pure, rhythms and
movements based, abstract style of dancing, with
no emotions or storyline. Whereas in Nritya, nrtta
is blended with **abhinaya** (a complex act – using
hand gestures, facial expressions, and delicate
body movements, to present a concept to the
audience), employing a Ras (of moods), and is
often used to convey a story.

Padhant: The act of reading out the rhythmic compositions (bandish) of Kathak and Tabla/Pakhawaj. Padhant is showcased to the audience during the dance recital, to help them realize the beauty of rhythmic exercises that the dancer is showcasing in their dance.

Panchakritya: The five functions of Lord Shiv. These are: **Srishti** (Creation), **Sthithi** (Preservation), **Samhara** (Destruction), **Tirobhav** (Concealment) and **Anugraha** (Providing Salvation or release).

Paran: Paran is a composition created with the sounds (or Bols) of the **Pakhawaj** (An ancient double headed percussion instrument that was invented in the Indian subcontinent. It is believed that it is the oldest double sided percussion instrument, after the **Damaru**, and was invented by Lord Brahma).

Parvati: She is the is wife of Lord Shiv and is one of the principal Goddesses in Hinduism. She is revered as the holy Mother. She bestows the Universe with creative energy, grace, nourishment, harmony, and devotion. She, along with Goddess Lakshmi and Goddess Sarasvati, completes the the **Tridevi** (Trinity of Mother

Goddesses).

Prana: Life. Prana is the force of nature that we hold inside ourselves to stay alive. It has to be constantly replenished with balanced nutrition, physical, and spiritual exercises.

Pranam: Reverence. The act of bowing head to show respect.

Pundit: An expert.

Raag/Raga: A musical framework or template created with musical notes. In Sanskrit Raag means color. Hence, in the context of music, Raag will depict a set of notes that are played together within a particular set of rules to create a specific mood or emotion. Seven major notes and five minor notes can be arranged in various patterns to create different Raags. A few popular Raags have been greeted and played with in poem #14 to express how they can be the most trusted allies through a creators day.

Ras/Rasa: see **Navaras**

Raudra: see **Navaras**

Riyaaz: Disciplined practice done daily to connect

deeper within one's craft.

Saadhana: Riyaaz

Sam: The first beat in the rhythmic cycle.

Sarasvati: Widely revered as the Goddess of knowledge and enlightenment, Ma Sarasvati (also, spelled Saraswati) is one among the Tridevi (see **Tridevi**). She is the deity who bestows speech, poetry, music, art and culture. She is the enlightened state in the supreme consciousness; hence, she is pure and divine truth, bestowing clarity and intellectual prowess. Sarasvati has been revered as a supreme deity since the ancient times of the Rig Veda. In the Rig Veda she is also worshipped as the river Goddess, in sync with the fertile ancient Indian river of the same name. Hence, Goddess Sarasvati was also associated with purity and fertility.

Goddess Sarasvati holds a Veena, rosary beads, a book, a kamandalu (holy water pot), has shimmering white skin, wears white attire and jewellery, and sits on a white lotus. She is escorted by the swan or a peacock.

In her Tantric form, she is Goddess **Matangi**, who also rules the fields of music, art, and knowledge (jnana). Maa Matangi also helps her devotees overrule enemies, unchastity, diseases, and foul company. She helps her devotee in obtaining the charisma needed to lure everyone to their craft and virtues. She is one among the ten forms of Shakti, popularly referred to as Das Mahavidya. Matangi, has a dark blue or dark green complexion, holds parrots, a sugarcane bow, sword, and a skull. She wears red drapes and a gunja seed garland around her neck.

Seva: Service.

Shiv/Sadashiv: Shiv (also known as Shiva, Mahadev, Hara) is one among the Trinity of primary Hindu Gods, alongside Brahma and Vishnu. He is the ascetic who is revered as the first Yogi (see **Yog**). He lives in Kailasa and is married to supreme Goddess Parvati. He holds the Damaru, the holy two faced drum that makes the sound, which creates the universe. He is the destroyer of evil and suppressor of malice (ego, avidya/ignorance). He wears the moon on his left forehead, Maa Ganga in his dreadlocks, and Vasuki, the serpent king around his neck. The bull is his vahana (vehicle). He is also worshipped as Neelkanth, due to his benevolent act of storing the extreme poison in his throat, in order to

complete the act of revealing Amrit (Ambrosia,
or the nectar of immortality) for the Gods.

In the field of dance, Shiv is revered as Nataraj
(see **Nataraj**).

Shringar: see **Navaras**

Surya Namaskar: A sequence of 12 Yog Asanas
(postures or stances) that flow, creating a
ritualistic obeisance to the Sun God.

Swara/Swar: Voice. Also, melodious notes.

Taal: Rhythmic cyclical patterns presented with
Bols (rhythmic syllables like dha, dhin, ta, thei,
tat, etc.). A taal contains a set number of beats
and bols with predecided accents.

Tandav: Dance of Shiv. Tandav can be Rudra
(violent) or Anandamay (blissful) encapsulating
the masculine energy of Shiv. In response to Shiv's
Tandav, Parvati offered movements of grace and
exquisite beauty. This version of dance, that was
created by the divine Mother is called **Lasya** and it
showcases the creative feminine energy.

Tantra: A yogic tradition involving texts, rituals,
and practices, that are focused on enabling

spiritual transformation of the practitioner from their gross state to a state of spiritual liberation.

Tatkaar: The sound of Tat that a Kathak dancer makes with their feet to play the Taal cycle on display. This element of the Kathak's ensemble showcases their rhythmic prowess and stamina.

Thaat: Stylized and graceful postures and attitude. The Thaat uses groovy movements using isolated actions of the **angas** (head, neck, chest, palms, sides of torso, hips, and feet) and **upangas** (eyes, eyebrows, nose, lower lip, chin, face, etc.) and briskly showcasing the Sam, while the Taal theka plays at the background. The Thaat element of a Kathak recital marks the beginning of the performance. It can follow an invocation act (like Vandana) and is generally followed with a set of brisk Uthaan pieces.

Tridevi: Trinity of Mother Goddesses. Goddess Parvati, Lakshmi, and Sarasvati, create this triad.

Upaj: Produce (literal meaning). In Kathak, Upaj is that part of the performance that is being done impromptu, unrehearsed, unchoreographed. The beauty of this element lies in its spontaneity that follows the bhaav (mood) of the dancer and their accompanying artists.

Urja: Energy. Vitality. Life-force.

Uthaan: A Kathak Bandish (composition) that uses light and simple Bols (Kathak words and syllables – e.g. Ta, Thei, Tat, Aa) to create ethereal compositions that feel light and blissful. "Uthaan – kahin se bhi uth ke halke se Sam pe aa jata hai" – Pundit Rajendra Gangani [They can begin anywhere within the Taal cycle but will land gently on the Sam]. It follows the Thaat during a traditional Kathak recital.

Utpatti: Source. Where everything originates from. In Kathak Utpatti denotes the neutral or the first resting position of the dancer. The feet are slightly apart, allowing the ghungroos to rest easy, the hips are square, chest straight, shoulders resting easy and straight, neck tall, chin parallel to the ground, lips in a soft smile, eyes looking straight ahead. The arms are in line with the shoulders – upto elbows, then bent to bring the palms in front of the chest. Palms are in "arala" hastamudra.

Veda: Vedas or Ved are ancient Indian texts that form the basic foundation of the Hindu way of living. There are four principal Vedas – Rig Veda (oldest veda; talks about religious rituals, family rituals, energies, virtues, philosophical questions), Sam Veda (root of Indian Classical Dance and Music, contains melodious hymns and chants), Yajur Veda (book of worship – it compiles religious rituals and mantras), Atharva Veda (guides on daily rituals of life; contains information on science, mathematics, medicine, etc.).

Veena: A stringed musical instrument that accompanies Maa Sarasvati. Veena is considered as the oldest instrument, as it was found mentioned in the Rigveda and Samaveda in the first millennium BCE.

Vidya: Knowledge. There is also a mirror concept "**Avidya**", which denotes ignorance of the ultimate truth.

Vishwaroopam: In Chapter 11 of Bhagavad Gita, Shree Krishna reveals his true form to Arjun.

Yog (also, Yoga): Union. As per ancient Indian philosophy, Yog can imply the union between the Yogi's mind and body. It can be the union between the Yogi's mind and their inner spirit. It can be the union between the Yogi's inner spirit and their divine creator / the Supreme Lord / the Supreme Spirit.

Yog is a vast subject. In brief, of the many paths to attain Yog, the path of "The Eight Limbs" or **Ashtanga Yog**, presented in the Yoga Sutras of Sage Patanjali, is most popular worldwide.

Yogi: The practitioner of Yog.

Zen: Becoming one with the Universe, or even a context, thought, or subject. Zen is a state of calm focus, where one has attained a Flow state. Their actions are guided by instinct rather than by conscious effort. Although, a Japanese term, the concept originated in China and spread South-East to Korea, Vietnam, Japan, and later worldwide.

2. Taal Glossary

Taal: A Taal is a rhythmic cyclical pattern presented with Bols (rhythmic syllables like dha, dhin, ta, thei, tat, etc.). A taal contains a set number of beats and bols with predecided accents.

Laya – is another important concept connected closely to taal in the rhythm of a composition. Simply, put it is the tempo or speed in which the beats appear in the composition.

At the base laya, the taal plays slowly. It is often termed as **Vilambit** or **Thah laya**. Usually, a Kathak maintains a base speed/ laya or 60 bpm (beats per minute).

A taal may be used in various speeds in a composition. Usually double and quadruple speeds are practiced in many complicated compositions, like the Kavitt. The double speed (120 bpm, with base laya at 60 bpm) is commonly referred to as the **Madhya Laya**. The quadruple speed (240 bpm, for base 60 bpm) is commonly referred to as the **Drut Laya**.

As already understood, a taal will create a rhythmic template with appropriate accents and dips in the beat journey of the composition. We can visualize a taal as the skeleton of the rhythm in the composition. There are many such templates that are prevalent in the Indian Classical Music genre, both Hindustani and Carnatic schools follow variants of similar templates.

Presented below are the basic Taal structure with bols and accents, popularly referred to as **taal theka,** for Taals used in the Kavitt series in this book.

Note: The beat numbers are shown as numeric as per sequence. The 'o' implies a khali (or dip) in the presentation of the Taal theka. The first beat of a taal is called the **Sam** and is represented with a 'X' or a '+' sign. Also, there is a double line symbol '‖' to denote the end of the Taal theka.

Sam: In Hindustani Classical Music, every composition should adhere to the chosen taal cycle, and should end at the 1st beat or Sam.

For example, if a composition uses a taal with 6 beats, the composition can engage as many taal cycles (repetitions) as may be necessary, but must engage: [6 times (any number) plus 1] beats, only.

Ashtamangal Taal: This taal uses 11 beats / matra.
Compatible with serene compositions that depict
the Shringaar (usually Bhakti) Rasa, or Veer Rasa,
or the Shanta Rasa. This taal may also be used
effectively to support Raudra Rasa in a
composition.

Ashtamangal Taal theka is as follows:

Dhi | Na | Dhi | Dhi | Na |

X   o   3   4   o

Dhi | Dhi | Na | Dhina | Kata | Kit ||

6   7   o   9   10   11

Basant: Taal Basant has 9 matra, and blends
seamlessly with happy and joyous compositions,
as well as compositions that invoke the Shringaar
Rasa. However, due to the stronger tail end of the
theka of this taal, Basant taal may also support
compositions depicting grave sadness. The unique
distribution of the beats in this taal make it apt
for moods involving ruthlessness and
stubbornness.

The Basant Taal theka is as follows:

Dha | Den | Ta dhet | Ta | Tit kata gadi ghene ||

X   2   3 4   o 6 o   8   o

Chautaal: Chautaal has 12 matra and is used in many Bhakti based compositions, invoking the Shanta Rasa. Chautaal is also amenable to bhakti (a part of Shringaar Rasa) especially when the devotee is enamoured (Adbhuta Rasa) by the magnaimity and grandeur of the subject being praised.

The Chautaal Taal theka is as follows:

Dha dha | Den ta | Kit dha | Den ta |

X 2   o   4 5   6   o 8

Tit kata | Gadi ghene ||

9   10   11   12

Dhamar: Dhamar engages 14 matra, and is often used in Dhrupad style of compositions. This taal is often engaged to induce the subtle playful emotions of Shringaar Rasa. It complements compositions that use light yet powerful descriptions of divinity and grace.

Taal Dhamar's theka is as follows:

Ka dhi ta dhi ta | Dha SS |

X   2   3   4   5   6   7

Ga di na | Di na ta SS ||

0   9   10   11   12   13   14

Jhaptaal: Jhaptaal uses 10 matra, and can easily depict many different emotions / Rasa. Shringaar and Hasya being its main consorts, Jhaptaal is a lighthearted taal, often depicting mischief or even mockery. In rare occasions, due to its ability to depict quick emotions, Jhaptaal can induce anxiety or sudden fear.

Jhaptaal theka is as follows:

Dhi na | Dhi dhi na | Ti na | Dhi dhi na ||

X   2   3   4   5   0   7   8   9   10

Panchamsawari

Panchamsawari is a 15 matra taal with a seemingly
complex uneven distribution of its beats.
However, this unique structure of this taal
renders it a playful and free-flowing mood as well.
Panchamsawari goes well with Shringar and
Hasya Rasa. The uneven texture of this taal makes
it suitable for energetic and textured
compositions.

Panchamsawari Taal theka is as follows:

Dhi na Dhidhi | Kat Dhidhi Nadhi Dhina |

X   2   3   4   5   6   7

Trikk Tinna Tirekite Tunna |

0   9   10   11

Katta Dhidhi Nadhi Dhina ||

12   13   14   15

Rupak

Rupak taal has 7 matra and blends well with compositions invoking the Bhakti Rasa, Veer Rasa, or the Shanta Rasa. It also blends well into celebratory compositions – like Bhajans and Kirtans. It is an interesting taal, which begins with a khali 'o', so the Sam 'X' coincides with the 'o', which may confuse some readers.

Rupak Taal theka is as follows:

Ti ti na | Dhi na | dhi na ||

0   2   3   4   5   6   7

Teentaal

Teentaal is one of the most used taal in typical bandish. It is versatile, easy to interpret, and blends well with any emotion/Rasa. Teentaal has 16 matra, and has an even flow throughout its theka. The taal structure is cyclical even within its base theka, with a distinct ebbing effect felt in its third section - beats 9-12. Due to this unique pattern of its beats, teentaal can create an energetic presence within a bandish.

Teentaal theka is as follows:

Dha dhin dhin dha | Dha dhin dhin dha |

X   2   3   4   5   6   7   8

Na tin tin ta | Ta dhin dhin dha ||

0   10   11   12   13   14   15   16